LIBYA 2016 HUMAN RIGHTS REPORT

EXECUTIVE SUMMARY

Libya is a parliamentary democracy with a temporary Constitutional Declaration, which allows for the exercise of a full range of political, civil, and judicial rights. Citizens elected the Tobruk-based House of Representatives (HoR) in free and fair elections in June 2014. The Libyan Political Agreement, which members of the UN-facilitated Libyan political dialogue signed in December 2015 and the HoR approved in January, created the internationally recognized Government of National Accord (GNA) Presidency Council (PC), headed by Prime Minister Fayez Sarraj. The GNA PC took its seat in Tripoli on March 30. A minority bloc of HoR members prevented a vote on the PC's proposed GNA Cabinet in February, and a quorum of members voted against the proposed cabinet in August, limiting the government's effectiveness. The proposed ministers, however, led their ministries in an acting capacity. The elected Constitutional Drafting Assembly's work has stalled due to infighting and boycotts by some members.

The government did not maintain civilian control over the "Libyan National Army" (LNA) despite efforts to persuade LNA Commander Khalifa Haftar to integrate into civilian-led governmental security forces. Some Libyan forces outside Haftar's command aligned with the government and joined a successful campaign against Da'esh in and around the city of Sirte. During the year the LNA, backed by the HoR, continued its military campaign against violent extremist organizations in the east, occupying cities and replacing elected municipal leaders with military appointees. Other extralegal armed groups continued to fill security vacuums in other places across the country. Neither the GNA nor the HoR had control over these groups. Da'esh maintained presence in the areas around Benghazi and Derna. Sirte was Da'esh's stronghold for most of the year, but a government-aligned Libyan military operation that started in May regained the city in December.

The most serious human rights problems during the year resulted from the absence of effective governance, justice, and security institutions, and abuses and violations committed by armed groups affiliated with the government, its opponents, terrorists, and criminal groups. Consequences of the failure of the rule of law included arbitrary and unlawful killings and impunity for these crimes; civilian casualties in armed conflicts; killings of politicians and human rights defenders; torture and other cruel, inhuman, or degrading treatment or punishment; and harsh and life-threatening conditions in detention and prison facilities.

Other human rights abuses included arbitrary arrest and detention; lengthy pretrial detention; denial of fair public trial; an ineffective judicial system staffed by officials subject to intimidation; arbitrary interference with privacy and home; use of excessive force and other abuses in internal conflicts; limits on the freedoms of speech and press, including violence against and harassment of journalists; restrictions on freedom of religion; abuses of internally displaced persons, refugees, and migrants; corruption and lack of transparency in government; violence and social discrimination against women and ethnic and racial minorities, including foreign workers; trafficking in persons, including forced labor; legal and social discrimination based on sexual orientation; and violations of labor rights.

Impunity was a severe and pervasive problem. The government had limited reach and resources, and did not take steps to investigate, prosecute, and punish those who committed abuses and violations. Intimidation by armed actors resulted in paralysis of the judicial system, impeding the investigation and prosecution of those believed to have committed human rights abuses, including against public figures and human rights defenders.

Section 1. Respect for the Integrity of the Person, Including Freedom from:

a. Arbitrary Deprivation of Life and other Unlawful or Politically Motivated Killings

There were numerous reports that pro-GNA militias, anti-GNA militias, LNA units, Da'esh fighters, and other extremist groups committed arbitrary or unlawful killings. Alliances, sometimes temporary, between the government, nonstate militias, and former or current officers in the armed forces participating in extralegal campaigns made it difficult to ascertain the role of the government in attacks by armed groups. In the absence of an effective judicial and security apparatus, perpetrators remained unidentified, and most of these crimes remained unpunished.

Reports indicated extremist and terrorist organizations played a prominent role in targeted killings, kidnappings, and suicide bombings perpetrated against both government officials and civilians. Although many incidents saw no claims of responsibility, observers attributed many to terrorist groups such as Da'esh, Ansar al-Sharia, and their affiliates. Criminal groups or armed elements affiliated with both the government and its opponents may have carried out others. Extremist groups using vehicles carrying explosive devices typically targeted military officials and killed scores of persons during the year.

The UN Support Mission in Libya (UNSMIL) documented 440 civilian casualties, including 204 killed and 236 injured from LNA military operations. Airstrikes caused the largest number of deaths, while shelling injured the most victims. On March 16, prominent civil society activist, Abdul Basit Abu-Dahab, was killed in Derna by a bomb placed in his vehicle. On July 21, UNSMIL reported that authorities found 14 bodies with signs of torture and gunshot injuries to the heads in a dumpster in Benghazi.

Da'esh fighters also committed numerous extrajudicial killings in areas where the group maintained presence. Human Rights Watch (HRW) reported that Da'esh unlawfully killed at least 49 persons in its stronghold of Sirte between February 2015 and May.

Da'esh fighters were driven from Sirte by the Libyan government's military operation al-Bunyan al-Marsous (ABAM). According to UNSMIL officials, ABAM fighters in Sirte allegedly tortured and executed Da'esh prisoners of war and possibly their family members.

Civil society and media reports claimed both pro-GNA and anti-GNA militia groups in Tripoli committed human rights abuses, including indiscriminate attacks on civilians, kidnapping, torture, burning houses, and forced expulsions based on political belief or tribal affiliation. In a series of incidents in Bani Walid on April 26 and 27, UNSMIL reported three Libyan and 12 Egyptian nationals were killed. On June 9, 12 former regime officials were shot and killed in Tripoli within hours after the Libyan Supreme Court ordered their release from the Ministry of Justice-operated al-Baraka prison.

Impunity was a serious problem. The government's lack of control led to impunity for armed groups on all sides of the conflict across the country. In 2015 human rights activist Entissar al-Hassaeri and her aunt were killed in Tripoli, and an investigator involved in the case disappeared. In the summer of 2015, judge Mohamed al-Nemli was tortured and killed near Misrata. The cases of Sheikh Mansour Abdelkarim al-Barassi; International Committee of the Red Cross staff member, Michael Greub; and human rights activist, Salwa Bughaighis, all of whom unknown assailants killed during 2014, remained unresolved. At year's end authorities had not investigated these attacks, and there had been no arrests, prosecutions, or trials of any alleged perpetrators of these killings.

b. Disappearance

As in 2015 government forces and armed groups acting outside government control committed an unknown number of forced disappearances. The government made few efforts to prevent, investigate, or penalize, forced disappearances.

Kidnappings were common throughout the year. On January 27, HoR member of parliament for Misrata, Mohammed al-Ra'id, was kidnapped for ransom in Tobruk. On February 24, authorities found an 11-year-old child dead in Tripoli after his family failed to pay the ransom. On March 27, anti-LNA activist, Ali al-Absilly, was kidnapped in front of his house at al-Marj.

Many disappearances that occurred under the Qadhafi regime, as well as many related to the 2011 revolution, remained unresolved. Due to the continuing conflict, weak judicial system, legal ambiguity regarding amnesty for revolutionary forces, and the slow progress of the National Fact-Finding and Reconciliation Commission, law enforcement authorities and the judiciary made no appreciable progress in resolving high-profile cases reported in 2013, 2014, and 2015.

c. Torture and Other Cruel, Inhuman, or Degrading Treatment or Punishment

While the constitutional declaration and post-revolutionary legislation prohibit such practices, according to credible accounts, personnel operating both government and extralegal detention centers tortured prisoners. At times during the year, due to its lack of resources and capability, the government continued to rely on militias to manage its incarceration facilities. Furthermore, militias, not police, initiated arrests in most instances. Militias, at their discretion, held detainees prior to placing them in official detention facilities. Armed groups also managed their own detention facilities outside government control.

Treatment varied from facility to facility and typically was worst at the time of arrest. Reported abuses included beatings with belts, sticks, hoses, and rifles; administration of electric shocks; burns inflicted by boiling water, heated metal, or cigarettes; mock executions; suspension from metal bars; and rape. The full extent of abuse at the hands of extremist or militia (government-allied and not) remained unknown.

UNSMIL documented cases involving deprivation of liberty and torture across the country, including in sections of the Mitiga detention facility in Tripoli, under the control of the Special Deterrence Force; in the Abu Salim detention facility; and in detention facilities under the control of other armed groups in Tripoli. Observers also reported similar violations and abuses in detention facilities in al-Bayda, Bani Walid, Benghazi, Khoms, al-Marj, Warshafanah, and Zintan.

Prison and Detention Center Conditions

Overcrowded, harsh, and life threatening prisons and detention facilities fell well short of international standards and were a significant threat to the well-being of detainees and prisoners. Many prisons and detention centers were outside government control.

According to the International Organization for Migration (IOM) and Office of the UN High Commissioner for Refugees (UNHCR), migrant detention centers, operated by the Ministry of Interior's Department to Combat Irregular Migration (DCIM), also suffered from massive overcrowding, dire sanitation conditions, lack of access to medical care, and significant disregard for the protection of the detainees. Additionally, many of these detention centers held minors with adults, and had no female guards for female prisoners. UNHCR reported an estimated 8,500 migrant detainees in the country as of March, although another humanitarian organization stated the actual number could be much higher.

Physical Conditions: In the absence of an effective judicial system or release of prisoners, overcrowding reportedly continued during the year. Accurate numbers of those incarcerated, including a breakdown by holding agency, were not available. A large number of detainees were foreigners, of whom migrants reportedly comprised the majority. Facilities that held irregular migrants generally were of poorer quality than other facilities.

The government urged military councils and militia groups to transfer detainees held since the 2011 revolution to authorized judicial authorities. Observers believed the greatest concentrations of such detainees were in greater Tripoli, Misrata, and Benghazi. Many facilities continued day-to-day operation under militia control.

Makeshift detention facilities existed throughout the country. Conditions at these facilities varied widely, but consistent problems included overcrowding, poor ventilation, the lack of necessities such as mattresses, and lack of hygiene and health care. Militias reportedly held detainees at schools, former government military sites, and other informal venues, including private homes. As violence escalated, the disruption of goods and services affected prisons, worsening the scarcity of medical supplies and certain food items.

There were reportedly separate facilities for men and women. In prior years in some instances, government-operated prisons and militias held minors with adults, according to human rights organizations. This practice continued in migrant detention centers and may have continued in prisons, due to the deterioration of conditions throughout the year.

These problems also existed in several migrant detention centers. Officials, local militias, and criminal gangs moved migrants through a network of detention centers. Reports indicated the conditions in most of these detention facilities were below international standards.

Administration: The Judicial Police, tasked by the Ministry of Justice to run the prison system, operates from its headquarters in Tripoli, but also opened a second headquarters in al-Bayda near the HoR. Additionally, many armed groups ran their own facilities outside the criminal justice system. The DCIM also operated its own detention facilities for migrants and refugees detained in the country.

There were multiple reports that recordkeeping on prisoners was not adequate and there was no known prison ombudsperson or comparable authority available to respond to complaints. It was unclear whether authorities allowed prisoners and detainees access to visitors and religious observance. Because there was no effectively functional judicial system during the year, oversight was problematic. Whether authorities censored prisoners' complaints submitted to judicial authorities was unclear.

Administration of prisons and detention centers continued to fall under the authority of judicial police. During the year the ratio of detainees and prisoners to the generally poorly trained guards varied significantly. International organizations involved in monitoring and training prison staff continued suspension of their activities amid continuing violence.

Independent Monitoring: The government permitted some independent monitoring, but the lack of clarity over who ran each facility and the sheer number of facilities made it impossible to gain a comprehensive view of the system.

Reports also raised questions about the capability and professional training of local human rights organizations charged with overseeing prisons and detention centers.

Due to the volatile security situation, few international organizations were present in the country monitoring human rights. While UNSMIL continued to monitor the situation through local human rights defenders, members of the judiciary, and judicial police, the absence of an international presence on the ground made oversight problematic.

d. Arbitrary Arrest or Detention

Following the 2011 revolution and attendant breakdown of judicial institutions and process, the government and nonstate militia forces continued to detain and hold persons arbitrarily in authorized and unauthorized facilities, including unknown locations, for extended periods without legal charges or legal authority.

The prerevolutionary criminal code remains in effect. It establishes procedures for pretrial detention and prohibits arbitrary arrest and detention, but both government and nonstate forces often disregarded these provisions. Throughout the year the government had little control over police and regional militias providing internal security, and armed groups carried out illegal and arbitrary detentions unimpededly. The lack of international monitoring meant that there were no reliable statistics on the number of arbitrary detainees.

Role of the Police and Security Apparatus

National police and other elements of the security apparatus operated ineffectively. The national police force, which reports to the Ministry of Interior, has official responsibility for internal security. The military under the Ministry of Defense has as its primary mission the defense of the country from external threats, but it primarily supported Ministry of Interior forces on internal security matters. The situation varied widely from municipality to municipality contingent upon whether police organizational structures remained intact. In some areas, such as Tobruk, police continued to function, but in others, such as Sebha, they existed in name only. Civilian authorities had nominal control of police and security apparatus, and security-related police work generally fell to self-constituted, disparate militias exercising police power without training or supervision and with varying degrees of accountability.

There were no known mechanisms to investigate effectively and punish abuses of authority, abuses of human rights, and corruption by police and security forces. In the militia-dominated security environment, a blurred chain of command led to confusion about responsibility for the actions of armed groups, including those nominally under government control. In these circumstances police and other security forces were usually ineffective in preventing or responding to violence incited by militias. Amid the confusion over chain of command and absent effective legal institutions, a culture of impunity prevailed.

Arrest Procedures and Treatment of Detainees

The law stipulates an arrest warrant is required, but authorities can detain persons without charge for as long as six days and can renew detention for up to three months, provided there is "reasonable evidence." The law also specifies authorities must inform detainees of the charges against them, and to renew a detention order, detainees must appear before a judicial authority at regular intervals of 30 days. The law gives the government power to detain persons for up to two months if considered a "threat to public security or stability" based on their "previous actions or affiliation with an official or unofficial apparatus or tool of the former regime." Affected individuals may challenge the measures before a judge.

Although the Constitutional Declaration recognizes the right to counsel, the vast majority of detainees did not have access to bail or a lawyer. Government authorities and militias held detainees incommunicado for unlimited periods in official and unofficial detention centers.

Arbitrary Arrest: Authorities frequently ignored the provisions of the criminal code prohibiting arbitrary arrest and detention. Quasi-state or nonstate militias arbitrarily arrested and detained persons throughout the year.

The government and militias continued to hold many prisoners without charge. A specific number was unknown, but observers estimated it to be several thousand. The government took no concrete action to reform the justice system. Gaps in existing legislation and the unclear separation of powers among the executive, judicial, and legislative branches contributed to a weak judicial system. Few detainees had access to counsel, faced formal charges, or had the opportunity to challenge their detention before a judicial authority.

Pretrial Detention: According to international nongovernmental organizations (NGOs), there were numerous inmates held in government-controlled prisons in pretrial detention for periods longer than the sentences for the minor crimes they allegedly committed.

While authorities must order detention for a specific period not exceeding 90 days, the law in practice results in extended pretrial detention. An ambiguity in the language of the law allows judges to renew the detention period if the suspect is of "interest to the investigation."

After the pretrial detention is ordered by an authorized judge, no appeal is allowed. This also applies to migrants charged with illegal border crossing.

Militias held most of those they detained without charge and frequently outside the government's authority. With control of the security environment diffused among various militia groups and a largely nonfunctioning judiciary, circumstances prevented most detainees from accessing a review process.

Detainee's Ability to Challenge Lawfulness of Detention before a Court: The law allows a detained suspect to challenge pretrial detention before the prosecutor and a magistrate judge. If the prosecutor does not order release, the detained can appeal to the magistrate judge. If the magistrate judge orders detention following review of the prosecutor's request, and despite the detainee's challenge, there is no further right to appeal the assigned detention order.

Amnesty: The government did not clarify whether it believed there was a blanket legal amnesty for revolutionaries' actions performed to promote or protect the revolution. It took no action to address violations committed during the revolution by anti-Qadhafi forces, resulting in a tacit amnesty.

During the year Misratans staged a series of high-profile releases of detainees in conjunction with the UN-led Libya Political Dialogue, as a confidence-building measure. The detainees included 300 former regime figures, including former head of State Security Mohamed Ben Nayil and Tuerga tribe members who had worked for the Qadhafi regime.

e. Denial of Fair Public Trial

The Constitutional Declaration provides for an independent judiciary and stipulates every person has a right of recourse to the judicial system. Nonetheless, thousands of detainees lacked access to a lawyer and information about the charges against them. Judges and prosecutors contended with threats, intimidation, violence, as

well as under resourced courts, and struggled to deal with complex cases.
Additionally judges and prosecutors cited concerns about the overall lack of
security in and around the courts, further hindering the re-establishment of the rule
of law. Courts in Tripoli continued to operate during the year. Throughout the rest
of the country, however, courts operated sporadically depending on local security
conditions.

Trial Procedures

The Constitutional Declaration provides for the presumption of innocence and the
right to legal counsel, provided at public expense for the indigent. During the year
state-affiliated and nonstate actors did not respect these standards. There were
multiple reports of individuals denied fair and public trials, choice of attorney,
language interpretation, the ability to confront plaintiff witnesses; protection
against forced testimony or confession to crimes; and the right to appeal.
According to reports from international NGOs, arbitrary detention and torture by
militias, including those operating nominally under government oversight,
continued to contribute to a climate of lawlessness that made fair trials elusive.
Armed groups, families of the victims or the accused, and the public regularly
threatened lawyers, judges, and prosecutors.

Amid threats, intimidation, and violence against the judiciary, the government did
not take steps to screen detainees systematically for prosecution or release. The
judiciary initiated very few criminal trials, largely because prosecutors and judges
feared retaliation. The courts were more prone to process civil cases, which were
less likely to invite retaliation, although capacity was limited due to a lack of
judges and administrators.

Political Prisoners and Detainees

Both government and militia forces, some of which were nominally under
government authority, held persons, particularly former Qadhafi regime officials,
internal security organization members, and others accused of subverting the 2011
revolution, in a variety of temporary facilities on political grounds.

The lack of international monitoring meant that there were no reliable statistics on
the number of political prisoners.

Civil Judicial Procedures and Remedies

The Constitutional Declaration provides for the right of citizens to have recourse to the judiciary. The judicial system did not have the capacity to provide citizens with access to civil remedies for human rights violations until the 2013 Law of Transitional Justice provided for fact-finding, accountability, and reparations for victims. Civil proceedings were difficult, with no courts functioning in Benghazi, Derna, and Sirte. Courts processed only a minimal number of cases in Tripoli, and there were continuous threats to justices and judicial police in all areas.

Impunity for the state and for militias also exists in law. Even if a court acquits a person detained by a militia, that person has no right to initiate a criminal or civil complaint against the state or the militia unless "fabricated or mendacious" allegations caused the detention.

f. Arbitrary or Unlawful Interference with Privacy, Family, Home, or Correspondence

The Constitutional Declaration considers correspondence, telephone conversations, and other forms of communication as inviolable unless authorized by a court order. Reports in the news and on social media indicated militias, gangs, extremist groups, and government-affiliated actors violated these prohibitions through the entry of homes without judicial authorization, the monitoring of communications and private movements, and the use of informants. Invasion of privacy left citizens vulnerable to targeted attacks based on political affiliation, ideology, and identity. Extrajudicial punishment extended to targets' family members and tribes. Armed groups arbitrarily entered, seized, or destroyed private property with impunity.

g. Abuses in Internal Conflicts

<u>Killings</u>: There were numerous reports that government-aligned militias, antigovernment militias, and some tribes committed arbitrary and unlawful killings of civilians. Primary targets of killings included political opponents; members of police, internal security apparatus and military intelligence; and also judges, political activists, members of civil society, journalists, religious leaders, and Qadhafi-affiliated officials and soldiers.

LNA Commander Khalifa Haftar's Operation Dignity continued during the year. The LNA continued attacks by ground and air forces against extremist forces in Benghazi, including Da'esh, Ansar al-Sharia, and their affiliates. While casualty numbers were uncertain, reports from media and NGOs estimated that Haftar's campaign resulted in hundreds of dead and thousands injured, including civilians.

Amnesty International (AI) also reported indiscriminant and disproportionate shelling of the densely populated Benghazi neighborhood of Ganfouda.

On February 7, an unidentified aircraft bombed the al-Wahda hospital compound in Derna, killing at least two civilians and causing extensive damage. Other airstrikes targeted the city that day. There was no claim of responsibility.

In April there was extensive social media reporting of disproportionate shelling by the LNA in Derna, which caused a significant number of civilian casualties and infrastructure destruction.

On September 20, an airstrike killed at least nine civilians including women and children and injured 20 in Sokna in Jufra. There were claims that either the Misratan air force or the LNA carried out the attack, but neither claimed responsibility.

Although exact figures were impossible to obtain, extremist bombings and killings probably resulted in hundreds of deaths. Terrorist organizations, such as Da'esh, Ansar al-Sharia, al-Qaida in the Islamic Maghreb, and their affiliates likely carried out much of the violence, although in many instances the perpetrators were unknown.

Abductions: Forces aligned with both the government and its opponents were responsible for the disappearance of civilians in conflict areas, although in most cases, the details remained obscure. In the eastern region, a campaign of killings, kidnappings, and intimidation continued to target activists, journalists, former government officials, and the security forces. Kidnappings remained a daily occurrence in many cities.

Over the past 18 months, Da'esh abducted and took into captivity at least 540 refugees and migrants, including at least 63 women forced into sex slavery for Da'esh fighters.

Physical Abuse, Punishment, and Torture: Jailers at both government and extralegal detention centers reportedly tortured prisoners. Militia control of most government and extralegal detention facilities obscured understanding of the situation.

The extent of torture at extremist or militia hands remained unknown, although some militias reportedly physically abused detainees. Individuals who expressed controversial opinions, such as journalists, suffered from violence. There were no developments in the case of Naseeb Miloud Karfana, a television journalist based in Sabha, and her fiance, killed in 2014.

<u>Child Soldiers</u>: There were reports of minors joining GNA-aligned forces, although GNA official policy required proof recruits were at least 18 years old. There were multiple reports of underage militia enlistees, but there was no verifiable information about any age-related requirements for joining. The government did not make efforts to investigate or punish recruitment or use of child soldiers. According to media reports, Da'esh claimed to have been training children in the country for its operations, such as suicide attacks, firing weapons, and making improvised explosive devices (IEDs). In April the LNA claimed Da'esh forced child soldiers from Libya and other Arab countries into a training camp in Sirte.

Also see the Department of State's annual *Trafficking in Persons Report* at www.state.gov/j/tip/rls/tiprpt/.

<u>Other Conflict-related Abuse</u>: Additional abuses stemming from increased conflict included restrictions on travel, deliberate attacks on health-care facilities, and the forceful displacement of civilians. Media reported armed groups involved in Tripoli clashes used IEDs in heavily populated urban areas. Authorities reported the same abuse in Benghazi, and on May 2, UNSMIL reported that an IED explosion in the al-Hawari district in Benghazi killed three children and injured one.

According to AI, under an LNA military blockade, hundreds of civilians, including Libyans and foreign nationals, remained trapped in the Ganfouda neighborhood of southwest Benghazi and suffered from a severe shortage of water, food, medical supplies, and electricity. On December 10, the LNA announced a temporary, six-hour ceasefire to allow the evacuation of civilians. Only a handful of civilians, however, were able to leave the besieged Benghazi neighborhood. The UN condemned the failure of the LNA to assure safe passage to civilians during its pledged cessation of hostilities.

Section 2. Respect for Civil Liberties, Including:

a. Freedom of Speech and Press

The Constitutional Declaration provides for freedom of opinion, expression, and press, but various militias, including those aligned with the GNA, exerted significant control over media content, and censorship was pervasive. Unidentified assailants targeted journalists and reporters for political views.

Freedom of Speech and Expression: Freedom of speech was limited in law and practice. The law criminalizes acts that "harm the February 17 revolution of 2011." The HoR, since its election in 2014 and the GNA since taking seat in Tripoli in March, did little to change restrictions on freedom of speech. Observers noted civil society practiced self-censorship because armed groups threatened and killed activists. Widespread conflict in major urban areas deepened the climate of fear and provided cover for armed groups to target vocal opponents with impunity.

Observers reported that individuals censored themselves in everyday speech, particularly in locations such as Tripoli.

Press and Media Freedoms: Press freedoms were limited in practice because increased threats, including abductions and killings by a range of assailants, including militias and violent extremists forced many journalists to practice self-censorship. These limits were present in print media, broadcast media, and book publication.

There were few reports of the closing of media outlets, but there were some reports of raids by unidentified actors on organizations working on press freedom. Indirect restrictions on press freedom imposed by both foreign and domestic actors further polarized the media environment.

Violence and Harassment: Reportedly, attacks on the media, including harassment and killings of; and threats, abductions, and violence against media personnel continued to the point where it was nearly impossible for media to operate in any meaningful capacity in areas of conflict.

Impunity for attacks on media exacerbated the problem, with no monitoring organizations, security forces, or a functioning judicial system to constrain or record these attacks.

While harassment of journalists was commonplace during the year, more serious crimes against journalists were widespread. There were reports of the arbitrary detention and torture of journalists. On July 29, authorities detained Libyan photojournalist, Selim al-Shebl, while he covered antigovernment protests in

Tripoli, but authorities released him without any charges after a few days of detention at the Ain Zara district.

In August, Misratan forces arbitrarily detained two journalists who worked for a major foreign newspaper and tortured one before releasing them without charge.

Unknown assailants killed several journalists.

On June 24, photojournalist Khaled al-Zintani was shot in Benghazi, and on July 21, photojournalist Abdelqadir Fassouk was killed while covering clashes between pro-GNA forces and Da'esh in Sirte.

On October 2, Dutch photojournalist Jeroen Oerlemans was killed in Sirte.

Kidnapping of journalists was also widespread throughout the year. In January media worker Abdelsalam al-Shahoumi was kidnapped from his workplace in Tripoli.

Censorship or Content Restrictions: The international NGO Reporters Without Borders reported that all sides used threats and violence to intimidate journalists to prevent publication of information. The unstable security situation and militia fighting created areas of hostility towards civilians and journalists associated with opposing sides. Additionally journalists practiced self-censorship due to lack of security and intimidation.

Libel/Slander Laws: The penal code criminalized a variety of political speech, including speech considered to "insult constitutional and popular authorities" and "publicly insulting the Libyan Arab people." It and other laws also provide criminal penalties for defamation and insults to religion. Most reports attributed infringement of free speech to intimidation, harassment, and violence.

National Security: The penal code criminalized speech considered to "tarnish the [country's] reputation or undermine confidence in it abroad." In view of the prevalence of self-censorship and the pressure and intimidation of nonstate actors, the government did not resort to its use during the year.

Nongovernmental Impact: The control of Derna, Sirte, and parts of Benghazi by violent extremist organizations restricted freedom of expression. Militias, terrorist and extremist groups, and individual civilians regularly harassed, intimidated, or assaulted journalists. While media coverage focused on the actions of Islamist-affiliated violent extremists, other armed actors also limited freedom of expression.

Reports from NGOs indicated various parties, including civilians, attacked journalists and media outlets, noting that lack of professionalism in the media sector exacerbated violence from those who disagreed with what media reported.

Internet Freedom

There were no credible reports that the government restricted or disrupted internet access or monitored private online communications without appropriate legal authority during the year. Nor were there credible reports that the government censored online content.

Internet penetration outside urban centers remained low, and frequent electrical outages resulted in limited internet availability in the capital and elsewhere. According to a World Bank study, 19 percent of the population used the internet in 2015.

The government did not exercise effective control over civilian infrastructure for most of the year. Social media, such as YouTube, Facebook, and Twitter, played a critical role in official and unofficial communications. A large number of bloggers, online journalists, and citizens reported practicing self-censorship due to instability, militia intimidation, and the uncertain political situation. Some activists reported finding what appeared to be "kill lists" targeting civilian dissenters on social media websites affiliated with certain Islamist militias.

Academic Freedom and Cultural Events

There were no reported government restrictions on academic freedom or cultural events. Security conditions in the country, however, restricted the ability to practice academic freedom and made cultural events rare.

b. Freedom of Peaceful Assembly and Association

Freedom of Assembly

The Constitutional Declaration provides for a general right to peaceful assembly; however, the government failed to provide for these rights. The law on guidelines for peaceful demonstrations fails to include relevant assurances and severely restricts the exercise of the right of assembly. The law mandates protesters must inform the government of any planned protest at least 48 hours in advance and provides that the government may notify the organizers that a protest is banned as little as 12 hours before the event.

Absent an effective security and judicial apparatus, the government lacked the ability to provide for freedom of assembly. The government failed to protect protesters and, conversely, to manage protester violence during the year. On May 5, according to the government, the LNA indiscriminately shelled peaceful demonstrators in the al-Kisk square in Benghazi.

Freedom of Association

The Constitutional Declaration includes freedom of association for political and civil society groups. In practice, however, the government could not enforce freedom of association, and the proliferation of targeted attacks on journalists, activists, and religious figures severely undermined freedom of association.

c. Freedom of Religion

See the Department of State's *International Religious Freedom Report* at www.state.gov/religiousfreedomreport/.

d. Freedom of Movement, Internally Displaced Persons, Protection of Refugees, and Stateless Persons

The Constitutional Declaration recognizes freedom of movement, including foreign travel, emigration, and repatriation, although the government has the ability to restrict freedom of movement. The law provides the government with the power to restrict a person's movement if it views that person as a "threat to public security or stability" based on the person's "previous actions or affiliation with an official or unofficial apparatus or tool of the former regime."

The country continued to serve as the primary departure point for migrants crossing the Mediterranean from North Africa, with more than 90 percent of those crossing the Mediterranean irregularly leaving from Libya. As of November 22, more than 168,000 migrants arrived in Italy per UNSMIL, with 4,164 migrants dying at sea. Boats were heavily overloaded, and there was a high risk of being lost or capsizing. For example, on October 5, 28 migrants suffocated on a boat off the Libyan coast that was carrying more than 1,000 migrants.

<u>Abuse of Migrants, Refugees, and Stateless Persons</u>: Some refugees and migrants faced abuse, principally arbitrary detention, but also killings and gender-based violence. Instability in the country and lack of government oversight made human trafficking profitable. Conditions on boats departing for Europe were poor, and human smugglers abandoned many migrants in international waters with insufficient food and water. Migrants reported some human smugglers were Libyan nationals, but officials did little to curb the departures or hold smugglers accountable for crimes against migrants.

<u>In-country Movement</u>: The government did not exercise control over in-country movement, although the LNA established checkpoints targeting extremist movements around Benghazi and Derna.

Militias effectively controlled regional movements through armed checkpoints. Militia checkpoints and those imposed by Da'esh, Ansar al-Sharia, and other extremist organizations impeded movement within the country and, in some areas, prohibited women from moving freely without a male escort.

There were also multiple reports of women who could not depart from western Libyan airports controlled by pro-GNA militias due to a lack of a "male guardian," which is not a legal requirement in the country.

Internally Displaced Persons

In August the IOM estimated there were 348,372 internally displaced persons (IDPs) in the country. Most of the Libyans displaced were from Sirte or Benghazi.

Limited access to towns affected by fighting between rival armed groups hampered efforts to account for and assist the displaced.

Approximately 40,000 members of the Tawarghan community remained displaced, the largest single IDP population. Because Tawargha served as a base for Qadhafi forces during the revolution, Misratan militias attacked the town following the fall of the regime in 2011, compelling all inhabitants, largely descendants of former slaves of sub-Saharan African origins, to leave their homes. During the year UNSMIL, with the help of the EU, sponsored talks between Misratans and Tawarghans to facilitate the return of Tawarghans to their homes. At year's end there was no resolution on their return to Tawargha.

On January 9, unidentified forces fired at least four rockets at two IDP camps in Benghazi, according to HRW.

IDPs continued to be vulnerable to abuses. The government was unable to promote adequately the safe, voluntary return or resettlement of IDPs. Due to the lack of adequate laws, policies, or government programs, international organizations and NGOs assisted them to the extent possible in view of the security environment.

Protection of Refugees

The IOM estimated that approximately 277,000 migrants and refugees traversed the country throughout the year, with the majority of migrants originating from Niger, Egypt, Chad, Ghana, and Sudan. UNHCR has registered approximately 38,000 refugees and asylum seekers in the country.

During the year UNHCR, the International Committee of the Red Cross, and the IOM provided basic services through local NGO implementing partners to refugees and asylum seekers. Despite safety and security vulnerabilities, humanitarian organizations enjoyed relatively good access, with the exception of Derna and Sirte.

There were reports that hundreds to thousands of sub-Saharan Africans entered the country illegally through the porous southern borders. Treatment of detained migrants depended upon their country of origin and the offense for which authorities held them (authorities held some for having improper documents and others for having committed crimes). Migrants and refugees faced abduction, extortion, violent crime, and other abuses, exacerbated by entrenched racism and xenophobia. Government-affiliated and nongovernment militias regularly held refugees and asylum seekers in detention centers alongside criminals or in separate detention centers under conditions that did not meet international standards.

On July 1, an AI report documented rampant sexual violence, abuse, and exploitation of migrants and refugees by traffickers, and criminal gangs. These human rights abuses occurred at unofficial and official detention centers and at the hands of Libyan coast guard and immigration officers.

Access to Asylum: Libya is not party to the 1951 refugee convention or the 1967 protocol, although the Constitutional Declaration recognizes the right of asylum and forbids forcible repatriation of asylum seekers. The government did not establish a system for providing protection to refugees or asylum seekers. Absent an asylum system, authorities could detain and deport asylum seekers without their having the opportunity to request refugee status. The government allows only seven nationalities to register as refugees with UNHCR: Syrians, Palestinians, Iraqis, Somalis, Sudanese (Darfuris), Ethiopians (Oromo), and Eritreans. The government did not legally recognize asylum seekers without documentation as a class distinct from migrants without residency permits.

Access to Basic Services: Refugees registered with UNHCR can access basic protection and assistance from UNHCR and its partners; however, during the year the government apparatus, whose health and education infrastructure is limited, did not grant refugees universal access to healthcare, education, or other services.

Stateless Persons

By law children derive citizenship only from a citizen father. Citizen mothers alone were unable to transmit citizenship to their children, but there are naturalization provisions for noncitizens. The law permits female nationals to confer nationality to their children in certain circumstances, such as when fathers are unknown, stateless, of unknown nationality, or do not establish filiation.

The Qadhafi regime revoked the citizenship of some inhabitants of the Saharan interior of the country, including many Tebu and some Tuareg, after the regime returned the Aouzou strip to Chad. As a result many nomadic and settled stateless persons lived in the country. Due to the lack of international monitoring, observers could not verify the current number of stateless persons.

Without citizenship stateless persons are unable to obtain legal employment. The government did not take action to alleviate the difficulties of stateless persons.

Section 3. Freedom to Participate in the Political Process

The temporary Constitutional Declaration provides citizens the ability to change their government in free and fair periodic elections based on universal and equal suffrage and conducted by secret ballot to assure the free expression of the will of the people, and citizens exercised that ability.

Elections and Political Participation

<u>Recent Elections</u>: In June 2014 the High National Elections Commission successfully administered the election of members to the HoR, an interim parliament to replace the GNC, whose mandate expired in February. An estimated 42 percent of registered voters went to the polls to choose 200 members from among 1,714 candidates. International and domestic observers, representatives of the media, and accredited guests mostly commended the performance of the electoral authorities. The Libyan Association for Democracy, the largest national observation umbrella group, cited minor technical issues and inconsistencies but stated polling was generally well organized. Violence and widespread threats to candidates, voters, and electoral officials on election day affected 24 polling centers, most notably in Sabha, Zawiya, Awbari, Sirte, Benghazi, and Derna. Eleven seats remained vacant due to a boycott of candidate registration and voting by the Amazigh community and violence at a number of polling centers that precluded a final vote.

During the year authorities held two municipal council elections, in the Yefran and Amazigha municipalities. As of June the LNA started a trend of replacing elected municipal mayors with military appointees. Ten municipalities in the eastern part of the country were affected as of October.

<u>Political Parties and Political Participation</u>: Political parties proliferated following the revolution, although fractious political infighting among party leaders impeded the government's progress on legislative and electoral priorities. Amid rising insecurity, public ire fell on certain political parties perceived to contribute to instability. In 2013 under pressure from militias, the government passed a purge or "lustration" law, the Political Isolation Law (PIL), prohibiting those who held certain positions under Qadhafi between 1969 and 2011 from holding government office. Observers widely criticized the law for its overly broad scope and the wide discretion given to the PIL Committee to determine whom to exclude from office.

Multiple members of the government claimed that it abolished the PIL during the year, but it published no legislation to that effect nor was it clear that the HoR had a quorum, which is necessary to pass any legislation.

<u>Participation of Women and Minorities</u>: No laws limited the participation of women and members of minorities in the political process, and women and minorities did participate. The Constitutional Declaration allows for full participation of women and minorities in elections and the political process, but significant social and cultural barriers--in addition to significant security challenges--prevented their proportionate political participation.

The election law provides for representation of women within the HoR; of the 200 seats in parliament, the law reserves 32 for women.

Section 4. Corruption and Lack of Transparency in Government

The law provides criminal penalties for corruption by officials. The government did not implement the law effectively, and officials reportedly engaged in corrupt practices with impunity. There were numerous reports of government corruption during the year but, as in 2015, no significant investigations or prosecutions occurred.

The Constitutional Declaration states that the government shall provide for the fair distribution of national wealth among citizens, cities, and regions. The government struggled to decentralize distribution of oil wealth and delivery of services through regional and local governance structures. There were many reports and accusations of government corruption due to lack of transparency in the government's management of security forces, oil revenues, and the national economy. There were allegations that officials in the interim government submitted fraudulent letters of credit to gain access to government funds.

Corruption: Slow progress in implementing decentralization legislation, particularly with regard to management of natural resources and distribution of government funds, led to accusations of corruption and calls for greater transparency. There were no reports of meetings of or actions taken by the Oil Corruption Committee, formed in 2014 to investigate both financial and administrative means of corruption in the oil industry.

Financial Disclosure: No financial disclosure laws, regulations, or codes of conduct require income and asset disclosure by appointed or elected officials.

Public Access to Information: No laws provide for public access to government information, and there was no available information whether the government granted requests for such access.

Section 5. Governmental Attitude Regarding International and Nongovernmental Investigation of Alleged Violations of Human Rights

While the government did not restrict human rights organizations from operating, it was unable to protect organizations from violence that often specifically targeted activists. Due to the government's inability to secure control of territory and the absence of an effective security apparatus, human rights organizations struggled to operate.

The United Nations or Other International Bodies: Government policy and practices were generally willing to cooperate with UN bodies, including human rights components of UNSMIL. Nonetheless, the government did not carry out UN-recommended actions to combat militias' impunity for human rights abuses. There were no prosecutions of revolutionary forces for war crimes during the year, despite official statements that it would not use the law granting amnesty for any "acts made necessary by the 17 February revolution" for the revolution's "success or protection."

The government also did not comply with injunctions by the International Criminal Court (ICC) to transfer suspected war criminal Saif al-Islam Qadhafi to ICC jurisdiction for trial. The government claimed that it was unable to obtain custody of Qadhafi from Zintani militia forces; to obtain evidence, in particular from witnesses who had been tortured during detention by militias; or to appoint defense counsel. In 2014 the ICC announced it had referred the country to the UN Security Council for violating an obligation to transfer Saif al-Islam Qadhafi for trial. In July 2015 a Tripoli court sentenced Saif al-Islam to death, but in the summer, authorities reportedly released him from house arrest.

Government Human Rights Bodies: Human rights defenders faced continuing threats and danger. The National Council for Civil Liberties and Human Rights, the UN-recognized national human rights institution, ceased its activity in the country due to intimidation in 2014 after armed men apparently associated with Libya Dawn militia forcibly closed its offices. The council maintained limited international activity with other human rights organizations in Tunis and the UN Human Rights Council. It had a minimal presence in Tripoli. Its ability to advocate for human rights and investigate alleged abuses during the reporting period was unclear.

The former government passed the Transitional Justice Law in 2013 (see section 1.e.), establishing a legal framework to promote civil peace, implement justice, compensate victims, and facilitate national reconciliation. The law further establishes a Fact-Finding and Reconciliation Commission charged with investigating and reporting on alleged human rights abuses, whether suffered under the Qadhafi regime or during the revolution. There was no known activity by the commission during the year.

Section 6. Discrimination, Societal Abuses, and Trafficking in Persons

Women

Rape and Domestic Violence: The law criminalizes rape but does not address spousal rape. There were no known reports of a woman accusing her husband of rape during the year. The Constitutional Declaration prohibits domestic violence, but it did not contain reference to penalties for violence against women.

By law a convicted rapist has the option to avoid a 25-year prison sentence by marrying the survivor, regardless of her wishes--provided her family consents. According to UNSMIL the forced marriage of rape survivors to their perpetrators as a way to avoid criminal proceedings remained rare. In previous years rape survivors who could not meet high evidentiary standards could face charges of adultery.

In early December a pro-GNA militia released a social media post that received widespread attention depicting a Libyan woman being sexually assaulted, allegedly by an anti-GNA militia in Tripoli.

There were no reliable statistics on the extent of domestic violence during the year. A 2013 report from the International Federation of Electoral Systems cited high levels of acceptance and justification of domestic violence in the society. Social and cultural barriers--including police and judicial reluctance to act and family reluctance to publicize an assault--contributed to lack of effective government enforcement. In the past municipalities and local organizations maintained women's shelters in most major cities, but it was difficult to confirm whether shelters continued to operate or were accessible to victims of domestic violence.

There was no mechanism to monitor violence against women and, in the absence of monitoring, violence, and intimidation against women largely went unreported.

Female Genital Mutilation/Cutting (FGM/C): There were no known reports of FGM/C by international organizations. There was no available information about legislation on FGM/C.

Sexual Harassment: The law criminalizes sexual harassment, but there were no reports on how or whether it was enforced. According to civil society organizations, there was widespread harassment and intimidation of women by militias and extremists, including accusations of "un-Islamic" behavior. Multiple local contacts reported harassment of women attempting to travel alone internationally at airports and in certain militia-controlled areas.

Reproductive Rights: Couples and individuals have the right to decide the number, spacing, and timing of their children; manage their reproductive health; and obtain information to do so, free from discrimination, coercion, and violence. Access to information on reproductive health and contraception, however, was difficult for women to obtain due to social norms surrounding sexuality. Continuing instability decreased available skilled medical personnel because many foreign health workers fled the country, which affected women's access to maternal health-care services and contraceptive supplies. The World Health Organization (WHO) reported that the large number of IDPs and access restrictions in conflict zones significantly affected the provision of reproductive health services. WHO also reported lack of access to basic comprehensive obstetric care (including emergency obstetric care and family planning) and treatment of sexually transmitted infections. According to current estimates by the UN Population Fund, only 29 percent of women between the ages of 15 and 49 used a modern method of contraception, and 19 percent of women had an unmet need for family planning.

Discrimination: The Constitutional Declaration states citizens are equal under the law with equal civil and political rights and the same opportunities in all areas without distinction on the grounds of gender. Absent implementing legislation, and operating with limited capacity, the government did not effectively enforce these declarations.

Women faced social forms of discrimination, which affected their ability to access employment, their presence in the workplace, and their mobility and personal freedom. Although the law prohibits discrimination based on gender, widespread cultural, economic, and societal discrimination against women continued. Sharia governs family matters, including inheritance, divorce, and the right to own property. While civil law mandates equal rights in inheritance, women often received less due to interpretations of sharia that favor men. Women may seek divorce for a range of reasons under the law, but they often forfeited financial rights in order to obtain a divorce. While the law demands men provide alimony for a fixed duration, according to the individual marriage contract, authorities did not uniformly enforce the law in instances when men failed to provide alimony. Women must obtain government permission to marry noncitizen men and often faced difficulties, including harassment, in attempting to do so while men did not face similar restrictions.

Children

Birth Registration: By law children derive citizenship only from a citizen father. Citizen women alone were unable to transmit citizenship to offspring. The country's nationality laws do not allow female nationals married to foreign nationals to transmit their nationality to their children. They permit, however, female nationals to transmit their nationality to their children in certain circumstances, such as when fathers are unknown, stateless, of unknown nationality, or do not establish filiation. There are also naturalization provisions for noncitizens.

Education: The conflict disrupted the school year for thousands of students across the country; many schools remained empty due to lack of materials, damage, or security concerns.

Early and Forced Marriage: The minimum age for marriage is 18 years old for both men and women, although judges can provide permission for those under 18 to marry. There were no available statistics on the rate of early and forced marriage during the year.

Female Genital Mutilation/Cutting (FGM/C): See information provided in women's section above.

Sexual Exploitation of Children: There was no information available on laws prohibiting or penalties for the commercial sexual exploitation of children or prohibiting child pornography. Nor was there any information regarding laws regulating the minimum age of consensual sex.

International Child Abductions: The country is not a party to the 1980 Hague Convention on the Civil Aspects of International Child Abduction. For information see the Department of State's *Annual Report on International Parental Child Abduction* at travel.state.gov/content/childabduction/en/legal/compliance.html.

Anti-Semitism

Most of the Jewish population left the country between 1948 and 1967. Some Jewish families reportedly remained, but no estimate of the population was available. There were no known reports of anti-Semitic acts during the year.

Trafficking in Persons

See the Department of State's *Trafficking in Persons Report* at
www.state.gov/j/tip/rls/tiprpt/.

Persons with Disabilities

The Constitutional Declaration addresses the rights of persons with disabilities by providing for monetary and other types of social assistance for the "protection" of persons with "special needs" with respect to employment, education, access to health care, and the provision of other government services, but it does not explicitly prohibit discrimination. The government did not effectively enforce these provisions.

The government did not enact or effectively implement laws and programs to provide access to buildings, information, and communications, but a number of organizations provided services to persons with disabilities. Few public facilities had adequate access for persons with physical disabilities, resulting in restricted access to employment, education, and health care. New sidewalks did not have curb cuts for wheelchair users, and new construction often did not have accessible entrances. There was limited access to information or communications.

National/Racial/Ethnic Minorities

Arabic-speaking Muslims of mixed Arab-Amazigh ancestry are 97 percent of the citizenry. The principal linguistic-based minorities are the Amazigh, Tuareg, and Tebu. These minority groups are predominantly Sunni Muslim but identified with their respective cultural and linguistic heritages rather than with Arab traditions.

The government officially recognizes the Amazigh, Tuareg, and Tebu languages and provides for their teaching in schools. Language remained a point of contention, however, and the extent to which the government enforced this provision was unclear.

Ethnic minorities faced instances of societal discrimination and violence. Racial discrimination existed against dark-skinned citizens, including those of sub-Saharan heritage. Government officials and journalists often distinguished between "loyal" and "foreign" populations of Tebu and Tuareg in the south and advocated expulsion of minority groups affiliated with political rivals on the basis they were not truly "Libyan." A number of Tebu and Tuareg communities received substandard or no services from municipalities, lacked national identity numbers (and thus access to employment), and faced widespread social discrimination.

Acts of Violence, Discrimination, and Other Abuses Based on Sexual Orientation and Gender Identity

Lesbian, gay, bisexual, transgender, and intersex (LGBTI) orientations remained illegal, and official and societal discrimination against LGBTI persons persisted. The penal code punishes consensual same-sex sexual activity by three to five years in prison. The law provides for punishment of both parties.

There was scant information on discrimination based on sexual orientation or gender identity in employment, housing, access to education, or health care. Observers noted that the threat of possible violence or abuse could intimidate persons who reported such discrimination. There was no information on whether there were hate crime laws or other judicial mechanisms to aid in prosecuting bias-motivated crimes against members of the LGBTI community.

Citizens tended to hold negative views of LGBTI persons and stigmatize homosexuality. There were reports of physical violence, harassment, and blackmail based on sexual orientation and gender identity. Militias often policed communities to enforce compliance with militia commanders' understanding of "Islamic" behavior, and harassed and threatened with impunity individuals believed to have LGBTI orientations and their families.

HIV and AIDS Social Stigma

There was no available information on societal violence toward persons with HIV/AIDS. There were reports the government denied persons with HIV/AIDS permission to marry. There were reports the government segregated detainees suspected of having HIV/AIDS from the rest of the detainee population, often in overcrowded spaces, and they received medical treatment last. In previous years there were reports of societal stigmatization of persons with HIV/AIDS due to an association of the disease with drug use, sex outside marriage, and homosexuality.

Section 7. Worker Rights

a. Freedom of Association and the Right to Collective Bargaining

The law does not provide for the right of workers to form and join independent unions, but it provides for the right of workers to bargain collectively and conduct legal strikes, with significant restrictions. The law neither prohibits antiunion discrimination nor requires the reinstatement of workers for union activity. By law workers in the formal sector are automatically members of the General Trade Union Federation of Workers, although they may elect to withdraw from the union. Only citizens may be union members, and regulations do not permit foreign workers to organize. According to a World Bank study in June 2015, efforts to reform labor legislation remained stalled due to the continuing political conflict.

The absence of an effective central government restricted the ability of the government to enforce applicable labor laws. The requirement that all collective agreements conform to the "national economic interest" restricted collective bargaining. Workers may call strikes only after exhausting all conciliation and arbitration procedures. The government or one of the parties may demand compulsory arbitration, thus severely restricting strikes. The government has the right to set and cut salaries without consulting workers. According to the June 2015 World Bank report, the public sector employed 85 percent of the country's active labor force.

Employees organized spontaneous strikes, boycotts, and sit-ins in a number of workplaces. No government action prevented or hindered labor strikes, and government payments to leaders of the strike actions customarily ended these actions.

b. Prohibition of Forced or Compulsory Labor

The law prohibits all forms of forced or compulsory labor. The government, however, did not fully enforce the applicable laws due to the absence of an effective central government. The resources, inspections, and penalties for violations were insufficient to deter violators. While many foreign workers fled the country due to the continuing conflict, there were reports of foreign workers, especially foreign migrants passing through the country to reach Europe, subjected to conditions indicative of forced labor. According to the IOM, militias and armed groups subjected migrants to forced labor and trafficking in IDP camps and transit centers that they controlled.

Armed groups prevented foreign health-care workers from departing conflict areas such as Benghazi and compelled these workers to perform unpaid work in dangerous conditions.

Private employers sometimes mobilized detained migrants from prisons and detention centers for forced labor on farms or construction sites; when the work was completed or the employers no longer required the migrants' labor, employers returned them to detention.

Also see the Department of State's *Trafficking in Persons Report* at www.state.gov/j/tip/rls/tiprpt/.

c. Prohibition of Child Labor and Minimum Age for Employment

The law prohibits children younger than 18 years old from employment except in a form of apprenticeship. It was unclear whether child labor occurred, and no information was available concerning whether the law limits working hours or sets occupational health and safety restrictions for children. The government lacked the capacity to enforce these laws.

d. Discrimination with Respect to Employment and Occupation

The Constitutional Declaration provides for a right of work to every citizen and prohibits any form of discrimination on religion, race, political opinion, language, wealth, kinship, social status, and tribal, regional, or familial loyalty. The law does not prohibit discrimination on age, gender, disability, sexual orientation and/or gender identity, social status, HIV-positive status, or having other communicable diseases. The law does not specifically prohibit discrimination concerning employment or occupation.

The absence of an effective central government also restricted the ability of the government to enforce applicable laws. Discrimination in all the above categories likely occurred.

Women faced discrimination in the workplace. Observers reported that authorities precluded hiring women for positions in the civil service and in specific professions that they occupied previously, such as school administration. They reported continued social pressure on women to leave the workplace, especially in high-profile professions such as journalism and law enforcement. In rural areas societal discrimination restricted women's freedom of movement, including to local destinations, and impaired their ability to play an active role in the workplace.

e. Acceptable Conditions of Work

The law stipulates a workweek of 40 hours, standard working hours, night shift regulations, dismissal procedures, and training requirements. The law does not specifically prohibit excessive compulsory overtime. The minimum wage was 450 dinars per month ($320 per the official exchange rate).

The law provides occupational health and safety standards, and the law grants workers the right to court hearings regarding violations of these standards. The absence of an effective central government restricted the ability of the government to enforce such health and safety standards.

Certain industries, such as the petroleum sector, attempted to maintain standards set by foreign companies. There was no information available on whether inspections continued during the year.

No accurate recent numbers of foreign workers were available. According to the World Bank, prior to 2011 the number of foreign workers was between 1.5 million and two million. The report estimated that (as of 2012) the informal sector employed 800,000 foreign workers (compared with 430,000 in the formal sector). Many foreign workers, especially in the health sector, departed the country due to the continuing conflict. Although foreign workers reportedly constituted more than 20 percent of the workforce, the labor law applies only to documented foreign workers with work contracts, who were a fraction of the total. While the law requires contracts for the hiring business to sponsor a worker for a visa, such contracts were rare.

The law permits foreign workers to reside in the country only for the duration of their work contracts, and authorities prohibited workers from sending more than half of their earnings to their home countries. Due to restrictions on converting Libyan currency into foreign currencies, it became difficult for foreign workers to send even half of their earnings to home countries.

Employers reportedly subjected foreign workers to coercive practices, such as changes in conditions of work and contracts, and such workers often had little choice other than to accept the changes or leave the country due to the lack of legal protections or avenues for remediation. Workers were not able to remove themselves from situations that endangered their health or safety without jeopardy to their employment.